The Holy Moly
Easter
Story

BY REBECCA GLASER

ILLUSTRATED BY BILL FERENC AND EMMA TRITHART

SPARK
HOUSE
FAMILY
MINNEAPOLIS

Contents

25 24 23 22 21 20 19 18 17 16   1 2 3 4 5 6 7 8 9 10

Book design by Toolbox Studios, Dave Wheeler, Alisha Lofgren, Janelle Markgren, and Ivy Palmer Skrade
Colorization: Dave Wheeler

Library of Congress Cataloging-in-Publication Data

Glaser, Rebecca Stromstad.
  The Holy Moly Easter story / by Rebecca Glaser ; illustrated by Bill Ferenc and Emma Trithart.
     pages cm. — (Holy Moly Bible storybooks)
  ISBN 978-1-5064-0256-7 (alk. paper)
1. Jesus Christ—Biography—Passion Week—Juvenile literature. 2. Jesus Christ—Passion—Juvenile literature. 3. Bible stories, English—Gospels. 4. Easter—Juvenile literature. I. Ferenc, Bill, illustrator. II. Title.
  BT431.3.G53 2016
  232.96—dc23
                          2015026222
Printed on acid-free paper

Printed in China

V63474; 9781506402567; FEB2016

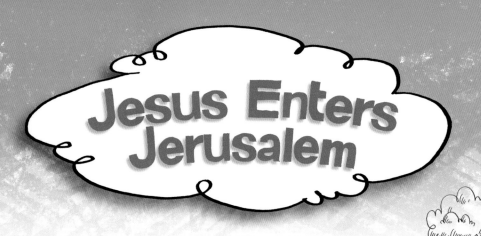

Jesus Enters Jerusalem

It was time to celebrate Passover in Jerusalem. When Jesus and the disciples arrived just outside Jerusalem, Jesus sent the disciples to get a colt.

Jesus rode the colt into Jerusalem. Huge crowds were there for the Passover festival.

"Hosanna!" the people shouted when they saw Jesus. "You are blessed!"

The people covered the road with coats and palm branches. "Jesus! King!" they cheered as they waved palm branches in the air.

Color the palm branches.

The Last Supper

The disciples prepared the Passover meal for Jesus, and he came to eat with them. Jesus knew it would be the last supper they would share.

Before they ate, Jesus washed the disciples' feet. "I have come to serve you. You should go and serve others," he told them.

They sat down at the table together and prepared to eat. Jesus looked at his disciples sadly. "One of you will betray me," he said. The disciples gasped. Who would it be?

Then Jesus took the bread, blessed it, broke it, and gave it to the disciples. "This bread is my body," Jesus said. "Whenever you eat it, remember me."

Then he poured wine, gave thanks, and gave it to the disciples. "This is my blood," Jesus said. "Whenever you drink it, remember me."

Color in the tablecloth.

After supper, Jesus went with the disciples to the garden of Gethsemane.

Count how many disciples went out with Jesus.

"I know that it is late, but stay awake while I pray," he asked his friends.

While Jesus was praying, the disciples fell asleep. "Wake up! Please stay awake!" Jesus said.

Jesus prayed two more times. Each time the disciples fell asleep. Jesus sighed, then woke up his friends. "Come, it's time to go," he told them.

Just then, guards arrived to arrest Jesus. The disciple Judas was with them. He betrayed Jesus by pointing out Jesus to them.

The other disciples jumped up to fight, but Jesus stopped them. "This is supposed to happen," he said, "so the words of the prophets will be fulfilled."

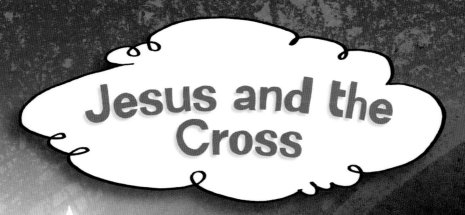

Jesus and the Cross

On that dark night, the garden of Gethsemane was quiet. The soldiers had arrested Jesus, and the disciples had run away.

The crowds were angry. They mocked and shouted at Jesus.

The soldiers had paid Judas thirty silver coins to betray Jesus.

The soldiers hurt Jesus and put a crown of thorns on his head. They forced him to carry a heavy cross.

"Crucify him!" the crowds yelled.

Jesus groaned and carried his cross up the hill.

The soldiers drove nails through Jesus' hands and feet. They hung him on the cross between two thieves.

Jesus gave a loud cry:
"My God, why have
you forsaken me?"
And he died.

Jesus' friends took his body, wrapped him in a clean cloth, and laid him in a tomb. They said goodbye, sealing the tomb with a large stone.
It was the darkest it had ever been.

The Empty Tomb

Mary Magdalene was sadder than she had ever been. It had been three days since her friend Jesus died, and she missed him very much!

Mary and her friend went to visit Jesus' tomb. They brought spices to put on Jesus' body.

But when the two friends
arrived at the tomb
early that morning, they found . . .

NOTHING.

The stone had been rolled away! Astonished and frightened, they looked inside. Jesus' body was not there. The tomb was empty!

An angel appeared. "Do not be afraid," the angel said. "Your friend Jesus is not here. He has risen from the dead!"

The two women hurried away to share what they had seen.

Suddenly, they stopped in their tracks. Jesus was standing in the road!

The women ran as fast as they could to tell the amazing news to the disciples.

Christ is risen!
ALLELUIA!

More Activities

LOOK AND FIND

Find the ___ in the Jesus Enters Jerusalem story on pages 3-6.

Jesus rode a young donkey instead of a big horse to show that he wasn't a prince of war but the Prince of Peace.

Find the ___ in The Last Supper story on pages 7-14.

Jesus said the words for communion that Christians still repeat today.

Find ___ in Jesus and the Cross on pages 15-22.

When Jesus was arrested, the disciples were scared about their own safety. Peter said he didn't know Jesus three times before the rooster crowed.

Find the ___ in The Empty Tomb on pages 23-30. It appears five times.

We talk about butterflies on Easter because of their life cycle. On Easter morning, the tomb was empty. When a butterfly emerges, the chrysalis from the caterpillar is empty.

ACTION PRAYER

Dear God,

Thank you for the good news!

JESUS IS ALIVE! *(shout with hands cupped in front of mouth)*

Help us tell others,

JESUS IS ALIVE! *(shout)*

WOO-HOO! ALLELUIA! *(pump hands in air)*

JESUS IS ALIVE! *(shout)*

Amen!

MATCHING GAME

Match the person from the Bible with the fact about them.

1. I rose from the dead just as I promised.

2. I was the disciple who told the soldiers where to find Jesus before he was arrested.

3. When I heard that Jesus had risen, I ran to tell the disciples.

4. I told the women at the tomb not to be afraid. Jesus was alive!

5. I was one of the first disciples to follow Jesus, but in the end I told people I didn't know him.

1. Jesus; 2. Judas; 3. Mary Magdalene; 4. Angel; 5. Peter.